【ミクコンセプト】

思考は思考をもたらす

思考は人生のすべてを支配します

際限なく閉じ込められた

Miku Suzuki

Kill Buddha

Meditations, narratives, poems, koans, enlightenments, contemplations, self-experiences, and aphorisms on Zen Buddhism, zazen, samadhi, ikigai, bodhi, karma, wabi sabi, self-discovery, selfishness, and Buddhas.

Bibliografische Information der Deutschen
Nationalbibliothek: Die Deutsche
Nationalbibliothek verzeichnet diese Publikation in
der Deutschen Nationalbibliografie; detaillierte
bibliografische Daten sind im Internet
über dnb.dnb.de abrufbar.

Herstellung und Verlag:

BoD – Books on Demand, Norderstedt

ISBN: 9783753472966

The days

1. The days

The days have passed and I have not always been happy. For years I was familiar with the wishes of the Buddhas around me and hoped to be able to absorb them and still think of them. Buddhas with hearts and well-intentioned joys did me good, and it was the whole new story to think about, or even more to think about. Always a new story, the old stories, new experiences and results did not exist, or if they did, it was only in my head. Drinking and eating remains, is good and has and quickly brings peace. So seen and believed in new stories, always believed. The thought that bit me has sharp teeth, the wound in the brain does not bleed. Let's make more beautiful stories. Nightmares don't need support. And the days have passed and a new day is here again. Time has me and that's good too. I am caught in the lies of stories and I stay in meditation and maybe that's why I love it. Are you me or am I just me in this story? I don't want to make it easy for myself, tomorrow will be different than today and the question is what remains. It doesn't matter, because everything is always new and the small parts of the present that are perceived shine differently than others, especially the good ones. Happy, that is a thousandfold beginning for all stories. Finding and trying. In the beginning, there was the pain that bored into my head and was also funny. Who could blame me for not being talkative and also thinking about enlightenment? The worst part was listening, nodding and pretending to understand. Doing something good for the other person, pretending to him that you have found a friend, making him feel that you are in good hands, and going crazy yourself. A constant lie, there's no end to it when you're trapped inside yourself. Saying goodbye to meaning is especially comforting.

2. Wealthy

Wealthy yet beside himself, the Buddha used fate as an excuse. Inspired by beautiful ideals, the next sense was recognized and properly polished, one must shine and that is a goal. The first young thoughts have become a strong tree that already bears fruit. Maybe it is the nonsense that keeps you alive, that gives you the taste and helps us survive. Prosperous, the Buddha in you and your destiny, everything shines and produces fat when fertilized. The earth drowns and artificial abstinence becomes part of this idealized world. It makes sense. The short sentence of the essential is abbreviated to death, it is accomplished, the hands are joined, the laughter hangs and the sad are right, what is it again, do you have me or what is or do we reject it? The sadness gets shorter, the sentence is finished and the smart ones make a nice rhyme out of it, the day has a sound, the night fear remains.

3. My attitude

My posture became more and more relaxed, the shoulders slumped and I could admire the other life, the other sun and the good monks. The bald head reflected the whole world and the nose turned against the wind. On what day did I not buy a pair of particularly beautiful glasses to keep my composure? The suns illuminate my other life and I am in love with awakening. Look into the near future when you grew up. Have you done well? Then you must have become happy. Breathing in made us pause. Heavy vapors fog our brains. Loss takes hold of me. Extraordinary days hit me. The crisis is beautiful. I am drunk. Everyone understands the past. The future remains - days and evenings pass.

4. Everything

Everything that is - is not true for me - and did not say anything - what is not there - we ask and we have one - and we guess - it is not in the I - I am gradually in the is - the day is tired and I am not there - and my mind is no longer there - it is only wasted in the brain - and everything is so good - it is just so, as you think - and the day is wasted again - look famous - crawl into meditation with praise - the future is different - we have won and yet have nothing - then it was night - the famous look has become different - the night is not always different - want and have - the writing has become smaller - and there is so much to read - well done and lost in the hand - everything is nonsense - try not to understand anything - go home and be the night.

The tooth

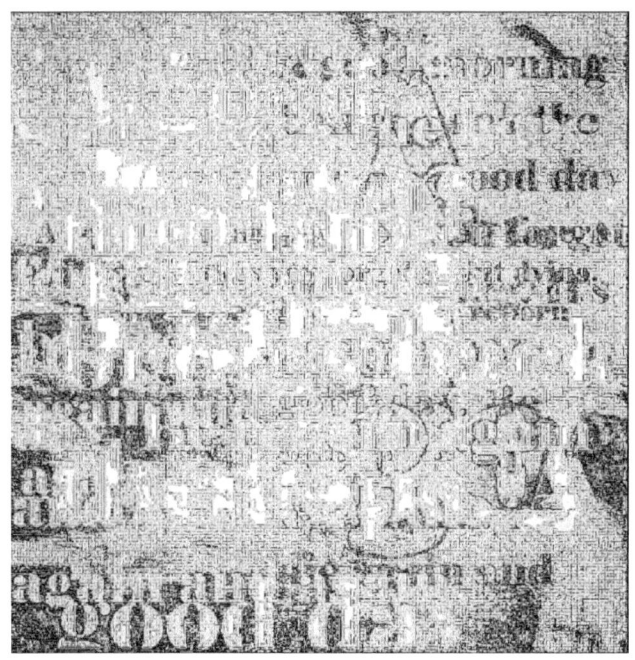

5. The tooth

The tooth of time gnaws at my consciousness, I hope for an enlightening subconscious and look for an opportune moment, I want to know what is coming and of course this will only mean something to me. The food tastes very much like a used towel in a public toilet, the tooth is full of holes and the exaggerated thoughts of Zen theater have no future. The donors were always nice to me until they stopped donating. I had wondered for years why? Was it a rediscovery of another level of consciousness? The ravages of time still gnaw and the root is broken. Confidence in the new madness ceases, the old has nothing and the new tastes boring and stale, declares it again and again, leaving the stomach hanging and wanting to belong. Hit the pain and you're in, a good joke, nothing to laugh at, but still a joke of the hopeless. In the evening I had a quick glass of liquor so I could see the Buddha clearly, and the Good Masters were there too, giving explanations of the main points of their worldview. I felt sicker than ever before. Being human is no fun without stories. And the Masters were talking and gesticulating and reliving the past. So the hours passed, and the days, and the years, and all of life. Nothing was really touched, why should I? Give me a kiss. Night has fallen, the candles glow to infinity, we sit silently and contentedly before the Buddha, thanking the Master for the stressful day. Everyone is thinking about their own future happiness or hopefully a few happy hours. A few dark figures fight their way through the darkness and appear black, the darkness drives the forgotten ones out of the loopholes, are they also looking for happiness or is it our fantasies drifting in the dark. You have a lucky charm in your hand, when the day is over, it will serve. Or are you already perfect?

6. Good sunday

Good Sunday, bring me a forbidden roast rabbit
and talk to me. We laugh at other people on the
street and don't really notice each other. Attention
is the magic word and love is next, love for the for
and maybe the against. Always the meaning is to be
mean and unsuccessful. The selfless is too difficult,
difficult and difficult or something else. A good
Buddha roast on Sunday, bread dumplings taste
with it, monks are happy and eat their way bravely
to dessert. What is difficult and what is soulful,
what is short and what is brave? And the temple
bells are ringing.

Especially today

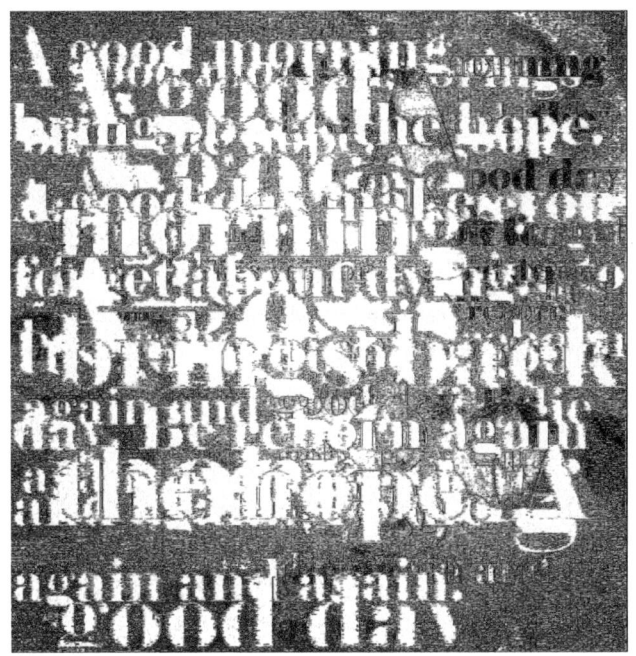

7. Especially today

Especially today I heard voices from the sky again, they wanted to tell me something, I don't know what, anyway it didn't sound very friendly. My concentration has decreased in the last years, too many sentences have challenged my brain cells and apparently some of them have perished too, or was it the bad air from the street or have I aged? Be warm and at least hope that you are loved, so you finally manage to ignore the curses and strangers or not. All are people, sick, troublemakers, murderers, angels, saviors and thoughts. Mostly to get used to everything and look deep into the glass. Too deep.

8. When a

If a vulgar text is peppered or you tend to withdraw, let yourself be touched or fear that you like it. What about the ordinary itself, loving it openly and being satisfied with it, is it an end in itself or a real satisfaction and are you? How dirty can you be that you still desire, what are your limits in your imagination and how tired is your aggressiveness? Constricted by custom and tormented by society, how are you trapped in your head, how are you without restraint. Respect is high and remains good. When wars come to you again, show yourself and tell us. And yet you lose yourself. Good, brave monkeys lie down the day after tomorrow in your hope for a better day and turn your attention to the essential. We believe and count on the day after tomorrow with indescribable discomfort and paint a picture of the restlessness we like or even hope to love, and even just a hope to love and fight like an animal, and we and the monkeys pluck and clap and live and they do not want to go.

9. In the north

In the north lies the cold, in the south the sun burns the day, there is a ring for the hand and soon the good man has nothing to say. And why? He does it so gladly and can enjoy his life in peace, drink the joy and put everything away. It is fortunate that there are Buddhas who help you to be weak, who help you to withdraw quickly. Mothers help, fathers suffocate, children scream and the water splashes, always a relationship we like, always a day like any other. Thank the enlightened and find the meaning or have you had enough of all the meaning, the boldness, the sayings, the aphorisms, the sacred teachings. The nest is empty.

10. The greeting

The greeting slid into my face, the ulterior motives of a better position just took hold of me, I hadn't been this focused in a long time, and yet nothing happened. The greeting subsided, I seemed a little more relaxed without surrendering, the ulterior motives were perhaps easy to guess. But everyone was in their thoughts and nothing happened. Persuasive, wise monks told of wealth and contentment, the novice relaxed his shoulders and believed for a moment. Quickly the past caught up with everyone. Rapture and slips.

11. The obstacles

The obstacles are getting bigger, the farmers are raising livestock for daily use and the enlightened people are complaining about stories from the gossip columns. The spring sun is already strong and warms the cold places in the city, albeit briefly, and evening is fast approaching. Quick questions come from very smart people and do not need to be answered. The peasants are good enough, because the beggars and enraptured cackle without end. Reproaches are a good way to anger the sensitive, crush the sentimental and weaken the strong. Being deaf is easy, you can't hear anything. Being killed.

There are friends

12. There are friends

There are friends who have fun - then there are hats with sense - friends protect themselves and are happy - people quickly go on the road - and humbly chase their dream friends - find each other on islands and say hello loudly - and stay and hold their thoughts - without intention - everything just happened - and the friends were lost again, no meaningful thought stayed with them - the hats have meaning - and they also have no meaning - the friends sometimes have a beard - and often no beard - some friends have beards and others rarely wear hats - and the roads get wider - the traffic gets faster - we hope for an island in us - with or without greeting - and the evening will come again - or old age.

13. The fertile soil

The fertile soil is prepared, the seeds of tomorrow's harvest are worked deep into the earth. And then waiting, waiting to see what tomorrow will bring, if pests have come, if the fruit will be devoured by thieves before the harvest, or if it's all just a game. A game that is about looking and having fun. And the picture becomes more and more blurred, spongy, faded or has dissolved and there is residue, no one wants to know. The rooms are getting bigger and the people in them more voluminous, the soil more sterile and the harvests richer. Pests have been given the coup de grace, what a mercy! The madness in the head looks like jewelry, the thieves laugh insanely in the meditation hall, also not to be there, not to have said anything, also not to be in eternity. Well-dressed human hosts take home intelligent tools to believe that business will flourish, because everyone needs a little Buddha, something pictorial, a spell, a magic. Everything goes well again, the games expand the horizons and, strangely, the trouble is gone. A fertile world of the mind. Sunbeams turn on my thoughts, bright moments briefly shake hands and tear off the nets, trees and bushes blossom and with them a whole colony of ants. There is enough to eat now, to eat, build up fat reserves on the unused fat that is there.

We believe that there is a good way out for everything somewhere, holy waiting, your Buddhas protect you. Countless Buddhas are buzzing around you and where are the illusions hiding, who wants to give birth to another one? Hopefully you are not an illusion and what about the Buddhas? Kill them, again and again, without end. The suns shine in your head and warm your skin, some even get hope and some get worried real fast. The bright moments reward you. Then come the great feasts and some gratitude, fat and death. Or everything will be fine.

Fun again

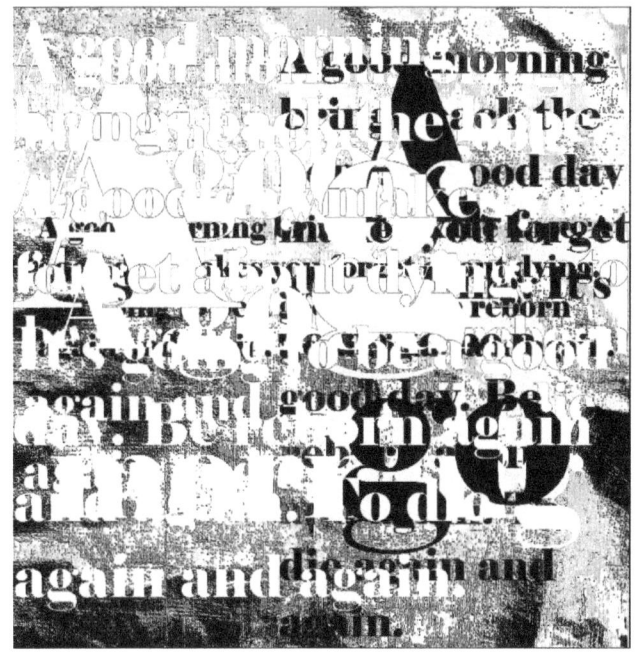

14. Fun again

Having fun again and can't get away from it - partying and needing to eat - what a wonderful life - well booked hours of fun - working and thinking up pleasure after pleasure - waiting for friends and being almost lonely - head filled with familiar thoughts - the beginning always comes new - nothing gets old - I ate it all and feel bad - and I can't stop, Having fun - buying hours of pleasure - making friends again - work makes a lot of sense - self - confidence is cultivated - something could be finite and tomorrow everything will be better - give yourself a lot of help with your thoughts - food is great fun - and finally do without. Funny you have seen - love is already hot and almost overcooked - and the heart is well cared for - I miss and I miss you - it's good that you have me - and you perceive me as pain - what is this stream - gladly seen and well felt - come to something and then you have me - am full of urges in meditation - seek the pain for a lifetime.

15. The daring ones

The daredevils take the short cuts - they look into the hearts of the available - want to use and kidnap you and me - the good guys meant it - and everyone thought - be superior - maybe they meant - or in the worst case they are inferior - the good noses of the daredevils - show more than moving hours - sacrifice more than good - I just did everything well - and were definitely used - stay available - the sense will grow and revive us - we were certainly well surpassed. You enjoy the conversation - you are a good storyteller - you have a big head - there is a lot of sense and hopefully emptiness - eyelids droop - thoughts are almost asleep - good killers come in - the performance makes tired - leads to new conversations - the voice is hoarse - my ear is closed - what is the conversation for - and - do you hear me - or - do I hear you?

16. Playful and well

Playful and well recorded, I learned essential
background information and can't really do
anything with it. The Zen Master is too phlegmatic
to start the day properly. They are well cooked and
starting to cool down. What has that, why don't
you go with me, what is that word in the throat, a
good beginning and a difficult end. Or not, we
know. And my legs carry me into the jungle of
thoughts, breathing heavily in the thick air, a
moment of happiness comes because I was once in
being and can tell about it. No one listens, the day
remains tired and the shadows begin to grow. It's
not meant to sound dark or anything. The counted
hours get their own smell, the bacteria do a great
job. Walk with me and get lonely with me, wash my
remaining hours and taste my thoughts, what
nonsense. But live the unity, no ifs, no buts, no
delusions, no you and me. None of it.

17. Our future

Our future is swimming towards us - only strong winners are coming towards us - we are searching almost fanatically for losers - we need support - a good grip in passing - what has become of admiration - when we are behind people - and when we are in front - the juice of life is no longer red - it is crystal clear and very thin - people are mourning for old friends - and we keep searching. I am in unfamiliar days - the new is always dear to me - the old is always new - looking for the state of fire - and the fingers become stiffer - the hips ache - the lungs breathe with me only half - and there is no more victory - or there never was - or there can be no such thing - what do beautiful minds actually imagine - nightmares are also justified - everyone has them - sometimes just sore - sometimes dirty - and sometimes well attended.

18. The words

The words make sense. And think about a next step in the meaning. Forgetting the words too quickly. There is a grumbling in the stomach. The food comes out of the mouth. The words float away. Lost in feelings. The taste reminds us of something, the pain in the stomach is not good, the loves are in the book, the imagination has captured us. The chants became louder and more beautiful. There was not a word to understand. Pressed my lips tightly together. And looked as skillfully as possible from my existence. Innocent. I felt. It's a great chance. And nodded. I nodded eagerly to you. And you saw it casually. Nodded eagerly and waved. Licked the master saliva. And nodded. A real nod. Moved out to meet the world, greeted many people, had meaningful conversations, the taste is sweet and I depend on it. A beautiful song resounds in meditation hall. Conversations have fallen silent. The saliva in the mouth tastes awful. The pleasure disappears.

The beloved

19. The beloved

The beloved moved through the country. The dress fluttered around the head. The underpants that didn't fit were showing. Going home and clearing your throat. Cradle your thoughts and lie sometimes. Soon you'll be gone. You played well and became known. Prepare yourself for the next phase. Become more solitary and patient. Good sentences are not lost. Wonderful taste. Breathe unsaturated. Borrowed thoughts. Liberated feelings. Bitten off tongues. Growing desire. A short laugh. Everything felt bad. Abbreviated path. Sweet taste. Crooked fingers. Healing prayers. Well adjusted. Gently dropped. Redelivered. Gnarled fingers grasp. The Buddha shines brightly. Cautious. Dive into the illusions. Another world is born. Modern wood smells pleasant. Be at home. And nothing else. I feel included, familiar and accepted, opinions are well received, everyone agrees with me and the stench creeps out from between the door cracks. The principles sound good and I can't really tell if I have enough, everything requires concepts, records and comparisons. I'm too lazy and unhappy for that right now. The spiritual things are coming and the world is almost endlessly full of words, how does that work? Keep the latest in mind and find new ideas easily. Have a good idea for the future

and grab everywhere. The toilet paper has been
used up. And the rule has been broken again. Come
here now and don't lift your leg. Inquiries are
welcome. Beautiful voices call for the neighbor.
Have swallowed well. Don't be aggressive and meet
again with others. The old day tastes terrible. And
do not recognize their own fears. You have pulled
out and smeared everything important. Happiness
is dissolving. And go back to the neighborhood.
Take a fear and despise yourself. Calm down and
swallow it all. Short inquiries are kind. Say it well.
Dress well and get out of here. Spit out the smart
sentences. Celebrate and dance. And again the rule
was broken. The silence at the beginning. Well
seen. Well aimed. Breaking rules. Insight. A theater.
Without. And at the beginning. And good.
Everything else. Without ifs and buts. The
lightness. No thoughts. Old master. Also a
beginning. He laughed for a moment.

20. Beautiful thoughts

Beautiful thoughts nourish the hero - crying
children express hearts - where is the happy
superficiality - and why do you add your little joy -
awakened heroes are celebrated and then
recommended - the monastery blessing hangs
crooked - thoughts become lighter and free - create
happiness for yourself - children cry sad and lonely
- all holiness disappears in meditation. I'm in the
broom closet - looking for a beginning - the room
is dark - the adventure is over - the broom closet is
not small - there are enough obstacles -
contentment is not lost either - the beginning is
good - the room remains dark - the adventure
becomes more intense - dialogues turn into quarrels
- are you alone - am I alone - the broom closet
remains at home - the singing sounds high. In the
very back is a haunted house - when will the full
moon come again - when will the moon shine on
the house - when will the glow be more bearable -
and in the very back of the haunted house - there
are the drunken screams of today - don't play
games - you don't need a game anymore - swim and
drown - and peace returns to the haunted house -
the ghosts may go to sleep - because peace is
appropriate there. You let go of everything -
everything crushes you - you are so free. Is it you -

and you see me - and you don't change - we embrace - and mean nothing - you think well alone - and you give yourself the comfort - opinions are good - opinions are bad - don't hide everything - go down slowly. The special moment has come - the hungry for life shake hands - there was nothing else - except sausage and bacon - a day like any other - many thought they had arrived - the complaints did not stop - many went crazy - questions arose - and no one was tied down - you were sent to the border into the unknown - interrupted and vomited - what remains is an empty stomach - and a new beginning. My heart, that shines - polished and good - shines deep red and pumps and pumps - I swallow well - and breathe rarely - laugh with strangers for no reason - if this is good - I don't know - I have lost my heart in my chest - it opened and no longer closes - my feelings suffocate me from time to time - but the sun shines again - part of the air is clean - another part is dirty - everything is well mixed - swallow well and breathe rarely - the heart remains red - and hopefully it will not turn blue.

21. Boastful

Boastful and well done, the earthly sense the outside and get stuck in the mire. Autumn will surely return before dark and we can think until we pass out and start a new day for us. A day full of old fears, there should also be hopes, there are beautiful inspirations and a pink icing. What is the trump card, who has the deciding cards, what does victory mean? What is it then? Be that as it may, anger makes the stupid scream and yet they know nothing. Fear grows and salvation does not come, all drift apart lost. Sunsets are part of it, passions are always reborn, beautiful or ugly, either way. A romantic song is sung in the head. There is no mercy. It burns long under the fingernails and the abbot grins, young servants make it easy and the hard-earned authority has a red face. Wounds are not only there to be licked, they also look beautiful, sometimes never heal and yet do not survive. Monks tie thick scarves around their necks and look thoughtfully in the air, they fart quietly and ignore you and themselves. And night comes and catches up with you, everyone is home. The stomach growls. The understanding was unrolled and read half the book in the bag, the surroundings slowly passed and the sounds became quieter. What was bearable and how, a fellow traveler asked the half-asleep dreamer. The grunted slightly, looked through his heavy eyelids and did not answer. If you understand for tomorrow and for the rest of life, you do not need more and everything is already explained. Or not. Sentences rattle into the gorge one after another and need nothing more. Travelers sing a hiking song and seek the feeling of unity, the feeling of togetherness and the successful thoughts that give the feeling of security. A few more are flooded with joy and do not listen, belong, take a break, find a meal. And the respect increases. Again a short thought comes to me and I cough quietly to myself, it can not really be a deep and long outpouring, the spirits do not bother me today, because my heart remains red and I hardly breathe. A special sentence. Unfortunately, my fingers do not find the light switch and I feel and yet find a soft piece of meat with buttons and breathe deeply and hear the deep red heart throbbing and somehow see it blue. I reach for a misunderstood poem and find the soft piece of flesh again, quite buttoned up. The ball is rolling toward us, the game has become serious business, and casual wear a uniform. We dream, we must dream, no matter what, want it and taste it, want the meaning that disappears, seemingly somehow and with your thoughts. The blossoms of the tree deceive us, the fearful rabbit could save himself and the brave died of a good deed. And run and run and run and fall straight into the grave, there was no point, it was the friendly day. The backpack becomes even heavier. What does the great infinity mean to the little seeker and how does he get away with it without knowing anything about it, it doesn't matter, the driven need him and nursery rhymes sound good. Are the thoughts easy to bear? My black robe hangs over the back of the chair, doesn't look good, doesn't look good anymore. My legs dangle hairily from the windowsill, they don't look good, don't look nice. The sky is blue, a few clouds pass through, it looks okay. My stomach is hanging on the windowsill, lying there, and I feel full. But that's good.

The fear

22. The fear

Fear haunts the wise and the rich - let yourself be caught and band together - there is a beautiful feast - you and fear and day and night - what comes - who stays - are we family - or is this the fear of the stranger without a home - I take you with me - and allow me to look - and watch me. A beautiful moon - it shines delicately through the dull brain salad - shines and we shine with you - the night is dark - and looking is not easy - families listen together - the moment comes again - the day is over. The sun is here - the cold is lost - the grass sprouts - the wind whistles through the bushes - there is the sun - the grass grows - people whistle as they pass - sun hungry they hold their faces in the air - a beautiful day - the rays bore into the train of thought - the wind cools the skin - thank you and over. A loving movement is often inconspicuous - the heart is clean - the lungs empty - what is screaming back there in the corner - not a bit forgotten - don't try to start - go home quickly and let yourself be loved - life is not always easy - the more you want - the harder it is for you - and you can't cope - all the conversations in your head are in vain. Children sing a song - spring is coming soon - or is already here - the beginning tastes sweet - the newborns wait patiently - the little finger shows nothing - well advised and guessing - day and night and the future - children sing a song - spring is getting old - the beginning is made - the beginning tastes sweet - summer is already here. Quick sense is quickly made - Lent also passes quickly - life is already over - the old have already said that sense brings us nothing new - the high mountain does not look high - the little things are often overlooked - the fast money trickles through the fingers - the moments pass quickly - what remains is a strange feeling - the open questions shrink - nothing is solvable - nothing is unsolvable - an eternal repetition.

23. Without sleep

Without sleep I can't laugh and I can't hit anything, without sleep I am completely lost and I don't take off either, especially the big things can't be seen and longing doesn't exist anyway. This is life without sleep. And I look for it and sometimes found it, nice and embracing, comfortable and safe, a good life, a life with sleep. Faces relax and kindness is back, tiredness becomes a good friend. And you have the sleep. In principle, it does not matter, we encounter desolation and do not dare to enter into a more serious relationship, it all does not matter and who wants to hear a true word? Those who say yes are permanent speakers, they don't care about you, they are closer to their dreams. But in principle and as a rule it does not matter. The word for this day has been said hundreds of times and is still useless. Time is in the armpit and the moment is also no longer fresh, the principles go bad, and further sayings can be saved. It turns out well, everything is bad. Now it is enough, the ideas are wrong and only copied, the armpits remain wet and will not be appreciated in the future. A thought on meaning. The toilet paper has run out. The greeting has arrived, the little master sits nodding on the throne yet close to the ground grinning and feeling good, the hint has come through and the speeches are not good for us. A good choice of words makes no sense, the urgent feeling of needing the meaning drives everyone crazy. Finally wanting to find a goal, but the talk remains, you're bad, I'm bad, everything is bad. And yet it is good again. After a short sentence again, without asking or paying. It depends on the right mixture, says the Buddhist wise thinker and represents me with his opinion, a good opinion. It depends on the right mixture of wine and water, it depends on the right mixture of thoughts, and the happy people talked about it. Don't get well again, not in this time, not in this life, talk that stays and mix the thoughts right. Change your thoughts, see everything as a game and say goodbye to seriousness for a short time. Dreams will come back and disappear. Resting on your rock, ask unreal questions and become free and unfree. The game makes everything a little easier. At least for a few minutes.

24. The little worm

The little worm crawls into the house, sets its plane everywhere and eats the most beautiful pieces that have been believed in. Sheer horror is reflected in the eyes of the meditators, one day the insight might be more reassuring, everything is gone, nothing is left. The cold night has made the meadow wet, worm tracks are easy to find and the beautiful dry slime speaks a flowery language. Everything that gave meaning has been eaten or has been destroyed, the enlightened cry in dark corners and no longer understand their world. They were destroyed, laughed at and from now on they are not well taken care of by their ego. Many things often come to a quick end. Exciting adventures are waiting for the crazy and disinhibited, well colored with poisonous paint. An old master laughs loudly and without restraint in his cell, the laughter turns into a scream, then into a grunt, and finally silence lies over the monastery courtyard. The students run wild, exciting adventures are forgotten and inhibitions spread. It was a beautiful day, the stones even smelled and the Buddhas gathered. Home becomes home, the shouting comes back regularly, the silence was already sacred. And the problems of life stories disappear anyway, when everyone forgets in death. At home you don't take in homeless people and protect yourself well in last steps or last ride or last night. It stings somewhere in my back and I can't see, my nose is stuffed up and my thinking is blocked, sense has cornered me and now wants the normal. When does the right story hit the mark, suddenly waking up and talking endless nonsense. Wake up and believe that I woke up. Count the sheep and glide carefree into the night again. Be crazy and wander, your heart beating wildly, wanting to get out and burst. The belief of having met other people just disappeared. Wind up the daydreams and then go out. Warm up, get hot and defy all odds, increase your fighting spirit, but it doesn't work like that, fight like a predator and everything becomes a sad game, because searching is not easy, especially at night. Where did you go, who stole your strong ego, where did it go and how can we find it again? Is it possible? Singing a song alone is not enough. And so it happened that nothing was done, because it is easy to forget.

25. The worst

The worst is - I don't know - I'm looking for it -
and I'll find it - the worst of all - the biggest mess -
I'll ask you - and maybe inquire - briefly touch - and
then eat - maybe eat. All is well and nothing comes
true - the grass that grows - the kindness takes its
place - and the fried brain tastes very good - the
past is rolled up - well lit and without shadows - the
words are collected - the flashes have been
abandoned - embrace me - and understand me - all
will be well - or is the end already coming in leaps
and bounds - the kindness is not a coincidence -
and the past gives you a reassurance - embrace me -
you can or you can not. A colorful bird fluttered in
the evening light - a sweet piece for all of us - a
cozy home is found - and there should be no
compromise - you have to find each other first -
and then nothing may be - an evening piece and a
morning piece - the night piece and the day piece -
art tastes good - good sentences are not lost. All
good - good beginning - affected students - broken
fingernails - black teeth - caught, caught listless -
happy to laugh - all is well - have loved well in the
beginning - broken teeth - black fingernails - good
words - no end - no beginning - have a new
thought. The Buddha for the poor - meditation for

46

the rich - let's put away our attachments - let's move the illusion in unst - sparkling stones - heavy dreams - we are balanced - and have nothing good. Since the heart is not yet fried - the hungry thought of yesterday is still here - the thought came from the heart - and I got hungry - wanted to devour a meal with meat - and feast - with heart and thoughts - hunger and roast - a new happiness - and the best greetings - the day is light - the hormones are somehow not in balance - everything has become good - hearts remain hungry - no real experience in the day - but good and a yes - take care of yourself - that was the rule that was always there. At least a laugh - no buts - good efforts - golden rule - a wink - a fence post - no if - and over - and under - nothing good - no buts - the weight - a short thought - little monks - the end too - a short laugh. The sound scratches the nerves - the nerves scratched with the poisoning - yesterday was today again - leave behind - there is no room for openness - the sleep is over - you don't look for a fight anymore - smart thoughts pass again - and some special thoughts set me free - I have been looking for a long time - and never found - joy has friends - and the nerves are bare - it doesn't matter and I am done. Celebrated naked bodies - torment their masses in the day - don't know what to do - doing good can mean nothing - always choose good words - the speeches become louder - the kings smaller - an insatiable worm fights its way through. Little by little and endlessly - a heavy

dream and a heavy head - have slept deeply - clouds
are moving - everyone can be happy - but
seriousness determines the day - join in and then let
go - the sense was passed again undeserved - the
sense was not caught - the other rests - this is the
beginning - black is the dream - the night is deep -
trust everyone - or do not trust everyone - serious
masters were laughed at - little by little, then again
immediately - there is enough to look forward.
Quickly seen - and throat tightened - yesterday, not
to have woken up - again found a good life -
quickly write down lies - we will invent a good day -
it will be well sung - the pleasure is far from over -
celebrate a feast - long wait - do not know what -
and we grow older - sing a song.

The day

26. The day

The day is getting brighter - security gaps -
everyone is looking for the center - you are having
fun - eyes are burning - joy is disappearing. Heroes
laugh out loud and know more - the feeling counts
- the favor lasted an hour - the news takes shape -
what does it have to do with you - where are you
going - we admire the beauty - we get lost in
feelings. The healthy is contagious, the beautiful
feeling is more than painful for us, but the
calmness took hold of us too. There I sat and heard
strange voices - I didn't understand a word and still
nodded eagerly - started laughing at the right time -
and nodded with a cramp in my neck - it was my
own fault - I thought to myself - I didn't
understand anything - don't know a way - and
nodded. But when I fell asleep while nodding - and
almost fell out of the chair - I felt an automatic
twitching of the neck muscles - politeness must be -
an honest nod is not necessary.

Round

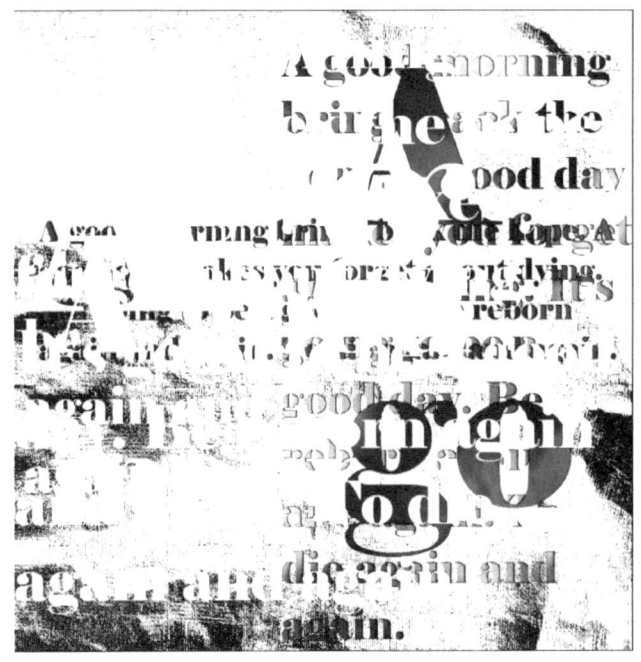

27. Round

Round and yet, thoughtful, spirits wrestling with each other, the day feels so simple. Brighten everything with a smile, grow together, grow through, grow up. Open and closed. We'll be there quickly, the answers will be found quickly, and we'll give fear a new name, the best one will probably be love, or the meaning of life, or the meaning of religion. Or. Advantages are easy to take advantage of and I always stand by the good, fighting murderously for the good. It is such a thing, too many again have a clear opinion. Everyone has a very strong opinion, because you are something and hopefully will always be something, pity exists only in the head and the smart ones at least think about it. You are something big and that is enough to have a clear and precise opinion. Serenity is not important, serenity has no place in the ego, you have to fight and then you become a respectable personality. Oh yes, just for whom. The great personality with a brain and a resume. To live on after death. It is also difficult to get up and enjoy happiness with your thoughts. Be fast and happy, be good enough and be highlighted. You are something. After many conversations and thoughts about Buddha and that you are getting closer to him, think about it again and forget everything quickly. Thoughts fly away and are hard to recapture. Every day should be a good day in the future, and the dream, hope and wishes remain stubbornly in you. So many things are funny, laughter and the beginning, the end also comes. In any case. Being caught in the environment, conjuring up important things, despising funny people, the environment is alive and we depend on it. I waited often and long, nothing came, I kept falling into the night and love turned into boredom. Waited a while, nothing came and the night became day. Tomorrow will come a new day, the old has also taken possession of me, and yet the restlessness will not go away. All experiences are good.

28. Hard sounds

Hard noises pass - a bird chirps in the middle of the head - the adventures are still ahead - people write history - the wishes of the remaining are great - maybe one more thought - the wish dies with - all is well and the master cries - you remain related - after all, it is the now that counts - now is no longer good. Forbidden time - suppressed boredom - slip into the good hours - do not enjoy without meaning - where were we - the shoe no longer presses - the pockets are empty - the shown joy passes - have swallowed well. A sip too much - a touch too little feeling - forget the inside - blur the outside - a sip too much - take responsibility regularly - and fall asleep. It has become more difficult - shake hands - wipe another's head - pierce other heads - to be nice - erase the past - or maybe not - it becomes more difficult - ears go deaf - feelings don't seem flawless - and still feel good - laugh from the heart - and - erase.

29. The day

The day is blue. The evening is sweet. The air is cold. The life laughs. Everything is getting shorter and shorter. A hunch emerges from nowhere. That, too, passes. The flash of inspiration quickly wears off. The room gets darker and the repetitions remain. Why not. Everything that is like that cannot exist at all. And there is another in me, a teacher once told me. We have accepted the search and made a good beginning. We ask and begin to have. And take the guesswork out of it. The meaning is not found in the ego. Gradually I have spent myself. I am wide awake and accompany the day. There are no meaningless hours here. Dream and feel a true spirit. Nothing has been done. Nothing is as imagined. And the day is wasted again. The saying is good, there is also a beautiful Buddha statue to see, bite your tongue and taste the sweet blood. Say it and listen carefully. Listen, take your thoughts and compare the long beards of the old people, they have turned gray. Sing a song in a particularly friendly way, you want to seem funny and maybe be funny, so you're somewhere in between. Since I fell asleep, I have not been able to get a word in, the thread is broken, the narrator's tongue is noticeably swollen and the words come close to me. It may be rude, but nature knows no excuse. The gray long old beards flutter in the wind and give a sublime picture, the old thoughts are still missing. Then the day would be perfect. The lecture is good and I like to be there, the sentence of the master sounds good and I write it down, hear it very often and remember it. At least I think so. The teaching is good and I am hammering the phrase into my head and enchanting myself. In the evening we run out of air and breathe heavily, examining all the details and finding no solution. The air has run out or it is too thick. Lie down, bathe in the sense, memorize all the sentences, keep them ready to fire, the right day will come. And if it doesn't, it won't. It remains a thought.

Flowers

A good morning brings back the hope. A good day makes you forget about dying. It's going to be a good day. Be reborn again and again. To die again and again.

about be a good again and again

30. Flowers

Flowers bloom in the garden - it shines brightly in the day - birds chirp and eat fat worms with relish - celebrate parties and never get too much - the sun shines in the hearts - there is always a lot to laugh at children - nothing can be heard in the distance - old clever people fight with their sticks through the meadow - roast themselves a sow and drink wine - that's what - that's good enough - flowers bloom in the meadow - children laugh, friendly old people instruct - worms are eaten - the day is good - and comes to an end. Teachings take no space - anger breaks out without restraint and no one calms down - fortunately there are whispers everywhere - crying becomes quieter and flowers sprout - the morning is red and in the evening you are drunk - beautiful thoughts come and stay - the beginning is made. Don't give up - just enter - harden the ego - anoint the fingers - wish a good morning - have a cozy evening - wishes are forgotten - the heart calms down. Nothing ever happens - nothing happened - have a good eye and be afraid - foundlings laugh loudly - the beginning is hard - there are many things in play - there is no certainty - and you win - or lose. The excitement has an end - the beginning is forgotten - the wise still talk about it - and the good has an appearance - go and tell a little - maybe about the good hours. Thoughtful but good - wake up and stare at the sky - the sky is so blue and bright - wake up and formulate the first thoughts - nature is loud and penetrates deep into the soul - is penetrated again for the first time and laughs - the view takes shape and I love it - take it all and unite. The evening mood and the aggression unite - the answers are near - the last day will surely come again - or not - it has a meaning - or a core - use the evening mood well - the aggression subsides - and it will be tomorrow. Come back. Without looking - I saw you - you gave a beautiful testimony - the smell of your worn clothes is in the air - pray briefly and send wishes to the sky - the optimists return from the battle - laugh wistfully - duck - be ashamed - the promise should be kept - just promised.

31. The sun

The sun has set, it became cold relatively quickly, the past faded. A lot of things came up in the conversations, especially those who were rarely allowed to talk, talked about the warm day and now said everything very boldly and did not really indulge themselves. So I listened and pretended to be wrong and very interested, my ears could not open and the brain said curfew. And the sound waves of the otherwise mute didn't really reach me. So I could make up all sorts of things, and I was too lazy to do that. The eternally old, reheated stories, they reeked of manure, there were no new experiences and the pants got tighter and tighter. What a dog, I thought, a smart dog that thinks like a cat and eats like a pig. The beneficiaries consider themselves lucky and really attribute everything to their talents. You have to be confident, train hard and tell yourself how to do it, then you can achieve something. And the know-it-all attitude didn't stop, there were just those who knew and I was and am a failure. Failure. Life goes on and thousands of know-it-alls are desperately looking for ears instead of thinking of a brain that processes at least parts. Answers are not wanted, discussions are not needed and understanding is supposed to be a joke.

A dog trying to manipulate me, a bastard eating like a nervous pig. The brain is bled, the greatest story is told, so please think about it. A well-made lie doesn't do anything in itself, no whirlwind will hit you, and you yourself probably won't notice it either. But the tender love in your tense heart is still looking for something, a piece of the coveted happiness. Everything will be different again, and the questions about when it will start will never end. It doesn't matter. Everything is always new, perceive yourself no matter what and you will shine like a fat piece of bacon, look inside yourself with joy and doubt. Find and try out.

32. Of course I am

Of course I have aged quickly without doing great things, but I still dream of the big day. No one can know what will happen to me and maybe to you. Our shopping carts have always been more than full, the indomitable are getting back up and are nowhere to be seen. The world has responded well to me, but never ordered or asked for anything in particular. There is nothing to ask, the expansion of consciousness does not tickle and who wants to discover the day with us? Time passes almost too slowly; it is impossible to catch up with oneself. As always, entrusted secrets are revealed and the most intimate becomes the joke of the day. The old also bring nothing, the young think of the moment or not at all and teach again and wipe and no longer necessarily want to be there. Hide well and no one will find you, a sadness, a laugh of a bystander, hope never dies, so they say yes. The horror came with the hangover, the toilet bowl was too far away and the hunger is probably gone for the next time, and the know-it-all continues to quickly watch over the essentials and is quick to joke. I feel sick. Terribly sick. Without strength there is no point in showing, and the lost one spoke faintly of the future. Everything slipped away, one pointed and shook his head. Give me a kiss. He lost himself in the darkness of principles, finally want to have enough land and gold, and often just stand and wait for the profit. Relying on good feelings, not to live differently and kiss the world just to have cleaned up. Since the fantasy went well, we could afford more than the average. Many congratulated us and cut our car tires at night. Good understanding is the basis of friendship. So I take off my hat and love everyone, meet friendly faces and reap great thanks. Thanks for nothing. Prepare well for the evening, make a good soup and take my notebook, read in it. That makes sense. Be off track. Look at yourself from a different angle. The benefits remain. Or does that make you happy, too? Nobody thinks anymore. Superiority becomes less and less important. We feel a burning in the back of our minds. And we sniff our way through. What else is there to show? Kindness and compassion? Want to be praised? Shout for attention. Always be ready. And be the beloved helper. Have done well for sure. Understand well and have a clear opinion, ignore the discarded monkeys for a short time, the trampled thoughts do not have to get out of hand, tomorrow is another day. We believe in miracles, miraculous coincidences and divine chance. The day after tomorrow will bring redemption, take heart and stroke your restlessness, fill your lungs with pure alpine air and look at your life. And like and love the image and fight like an opinion maker, believe in values and do not see crazy monkeys as brothers. We mean it and we need it very much, and yet we will disappear too quickly.

Take care

33. Take care

Take care of yourself. Don't let yourself get hurt. I
don't have a head. For all the thoughts. You sing a
song and fly through the air. Describe good words.
The words hit straight to the heart. Draw attention
to yourself. There is much to hear. Unfortunately,
the ear is closed. Conversations linger. And. Do
you see me? Or I hear you. You're already a little
crazy, kneading old wounds and suddenly get up
and leave, everything has become too much and
self-sacrifice needs no discipline, be proud of it, stir
in the dirt at home, curse your mother and lie
awake endlessly with her thick blanket. Open your
head and ask what's wrong, the heavy blanket
squeezes the air out of you and you stammer about
freedom, the madness becomes more intense in
you, the sentences longer and the music before bed
sounds good. Slowly you fall asleep, the will
remains. And you sometimes get lost. What is the
truth? Have you encountered the truth while
walking? There's just nothing left of dirt and shine.
The answers you want are harder. Always
reinvented. Have not consciously lied. Don't even
know the truth. And sometimes get lost. The days
are over. Once again. Find meaning in tomorrow's
days. There's nothing left of the profit. And the

night fell. The all-knowing gaze became fixed. The night brought cool air. The wish was not really granted. The text was misunderstood. And there is nothing more to read. So everything goes round in circles. Well called. All have understood. Go home and be the night. I ran at full speed, forgetting my stomach and beaming in tired faces, our togetherness is promoted, the good and reasonable education. Aging is no longer important, and the hardened lower legs do not remain free of varicose veins. Where is the world going? I will be there. My sense has a wide illusion and the day is spoiled, I don't mind the sun and I am ready for more humiliation. Look into the near future when you wake up.

34. Summarize the day

Summarize the day extra briefly, accidentally swat a fly and feel uncomfortable. What comes out of the shallows, you are a thinker. Tired of worrying. Playing too well. Believe in the beginning and the end. Love deep in the heart. Justice is the most important thing. Play with the days, time passes. And death comes with you. The butt itches. Hear a familiar laugh. I pocket the having. The end is already near. Pleasure foams away. Loves are lost. Bleeding hearts are seen. Forgotten is the balanced absence. I am trapped in myself and in thoughts. Pain enchants the day. Feel the end weak. Good feelings are not always good. Be a better person and choose me. To lead with the basest instincts is the art. And shout out the pain of life. When you give up, I believe. It's a mindful flight. Or have you seen me and are you popular too? The dirty fingernails just don't look good and thinking about thinking doesn't do any good and the cleanliness fades and you can go back to worrying about the future or are there also opposing voices in you and you've always been and you always want to give up and you give all of yourself and you are. The pig goes home. The child grows older. The great master falls apart. Caresses are exchanged.

Accepted and lost. Greetings and a warm welcome. The worms eat through your head. The sacred song grows quieter. Where are they? Are they already asleep? They disappear into the darkness. Everything seems quiet and lonely. You can't change it. I've already eaten my fill and I'm still hungry for more, my stomach is already full but my tongue is licking for more. There's something nice about family gatherings. My grandma chatting excitedly with other people. My grandma is resting in the cemetery and the cooked beef tastes horrible as usual. The days are coming and the earth will be your final resting place. Maybe desserts won't be eaten then and maybe the children will laugh even louder than they do now. Don't be sentimental, there will be nothing left of you and the next ones will need space. And the temple bell will ring.

35. The day

The day has not started for a long time. At least I think so. The shoes press on the toes. They should be one size too tight. It hurts and distracts me. My face is spinning. And you apologize for your problems. There is no meeting. Come here and give me a hug. It won't do any good, but it's nice. Make friends and find something good in life. Time passes quickly. And you still can't catch anything. I've always hoped. Explore again have a lot of the day. And sometimes you get visitors. What do you want to understand, nature's system or your favorite counterpart, or at least reach into your backpack yourself and get out your snack pack. You'll find the right pattern and you won't want to do anything with it. Use the trick of different perspectives and slip from one person to another. As if that's your end in itself, start singing a nice song, show them almost naked and they'll still ignore you. Then you run and grab as much luggage as you can to have more with you and are glad you hoarded it. I tie myself up and ask everyone in this confinement and hear nothing, but I do not feel uncomfortable. The I seems beautiful and believes again in the higher, like everyone else, and in understanding and happiness. And yet one loses oneself. One suffocates. The skin becomes cold. The tip of the nose slowly turns blue. The day tastes sweet. Love gives itself to me. Can't stand anything more. We find it hard to have an opinion. The smell becomes more intense and corrosive. A shiver goes diagonally over the viewer. Opinions come to life. The sweat tastes disgusting. And one is dead. After much conversation, I fell asleep trying to come to terms with the new truths. I also wanted to say something, but no one listened to me or said anything about my opinion. The deep sleep recovered me and the voices became quieter, actually I didn't understand anything anymore, but I still wanted to talk and be there. Many sentences were said, especially about the right behavior to understand others better. I also felt sick from the bottom up, from the wet lips and the spit flying through the air. Can't take care of the kindness I was hoping for, sleep is the best cure. Take a sip of poison, I feel sick, and look at the pile of words kindly and deeply. Too deep.

36. At last

At last a thought with meaning emerges, very briefly and quietly, fleeing and emptying the mind and taking a deep breath and giving life an artificial meaning. The piano drones in the neighboring apartment. The neighbors turn up their voices. Discussions are heated up. If you have strong feelings, you belong. Let yourself be celebrated and you will be a hero. Look at all the faces and say yes. The next day will come. And happiness can be small again. You give yourself a new day. All holiness disappears in meditation. When I fall over and gasp in the floor, briefly discuss but somehow not heard, my mouth chews wet mud, the day sounds joyful in my heart and lying down suits me, my fingers drill holes in the floor and the day is now done. The chest feels constricted, some things are not cleared and spread from the stomach to the throat, there will be a beginning again and I treat myself to an ice cream. Greetings are no longer my habit, dialogues leave a bad taste and yet I become more relaxed. My ulterior motives drown in the swamp of many views, but I still lick the ice cream with relish and wonder if the anxiety will subside. Tomorrow, perhaps, it will be possible to take a deep breath and make new life plans. Take a deep breath and hatch. I run around shouting funny sayings at colleagues, posture relaxes a little, running makes you tired. No one can see if the oven is still on or already off, but it will definitely be hotter. I still listened and was amazed at the rhymed statements and crude sayings. My stomach growled and hunger ruled my head. This is how the madness should begin, important things in the environment and a small dominant thing. A good start in this environment. The goodbyes are especially comforting. The ear was clogged by the many words. The mouths move towards you. I don't know what tomorrow is. The affection is also an affection. Get up again. Everything has a meaning. We have enclosed everything new in our hearts. Come here and find my happiness. I am happy to give you a piece. You were fed for many hours and you were hungry. I will not be full today. There is no end to thirst either. We humans let off steam. Thunderstorms do not irritate us. The nose was beaten bloody. And the shouting gets on our nerves. All friends have been lost.

37. From being

Spoiled by being, I often confess to appearances and make new plans, there's a mountain I'm going to climb and then I'm going to understand myself or not and I'm here rubbing the dirt out of the spaces between my toes and I'm happy. You lie frozen in the trickle and count your fingers, they are all there and you look tired. The night was cold, the encounters were unsuccessful and the spirit of wine weighed on me, there was not much to say. I really enjoyed it and I'm proud of it, I really drank and I'm proud of it. Proud, very proud and happy. Well-rehearsed days judge us and find the freedom so good to drink and eat and be a pig. The relationships that please and the big gulp, the right to stay, make you faithful. Buddhist sense finders break up and bite their nails, orders to follow, and laugh for the rest of the day. Stagger home cold, looking for the door key. The nest is empty. The dog has peed on your leg. The sex hangs heavy. The wetness takes the cold with it. Your sense and faith crumble quickly. The leg becomes less important. You run into your wall. And you beat your nose bloody. All beginnings are hard. Slowly your pants dry. And slowly the blood dries on your face. The conversations get louder again. Everyone comes together. And talk wildly to each other. The past disappears. The singing rings high. Choppy spinning lies in the bowl for the daily meal. Vanity proliferates and produces thick ulcers, the sun grills the brown raised facial contours black. It gets cold on the back where no one can look, and all questions are quickly answered, nothing is owed to us, everything depends on a good opinion or you firmly believe in a good opinion. You don't have to close your heart, be ready for all feelings, because I want to say that I live and also stumble. But be vain and let yourself be blackened and take a deep breath. Spit the phlegm from your lungs, everything is not as we thought. Kill Buddha at last. Spit on the face. Cake sticks to butt cheeks. I grunted and smile at my master. We're fraternizing fast now. Time has done nothing to us. Who's going to be mad right away? How are you? How well can you wait?

We will see

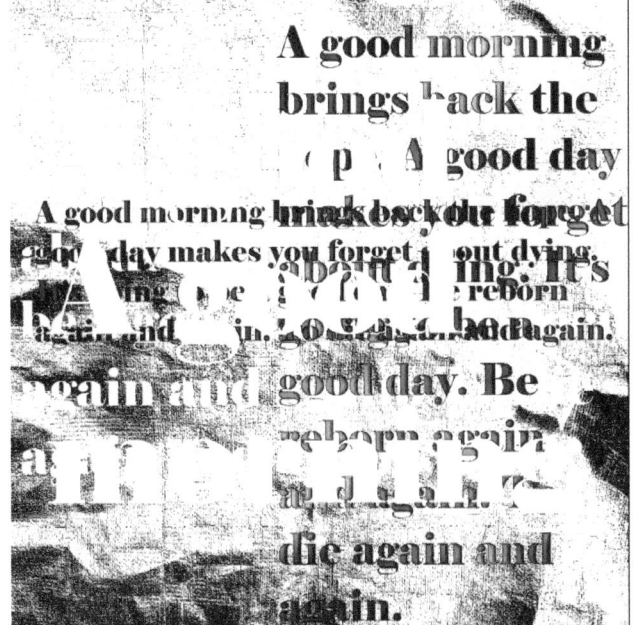

38. We will see

We will see. What will make us happy? Do you
want to breathe deeply again one day? The drugs
dampen us. Nothing to lose. Everything stays as it
is. We meet in neutral spaces. Wake up and be
mine. There is nothing to understand. All times
extinguish. The days and evenings die out. The
drunkards join together and have come up with
new goals, want to be respected and create
everything, are in the right place and take you with
them and know no mercy, crazy and normal and
entangled. Have a good idea of the beautiful,
especially tall and slim and then funny and nice and
then young and unassuming and best heard. The
swamp affects us all, he said, and he is still stuck.
The good character was quickly forgotten and with
it the strong personality that this character became.
You suck in the leaden air and nod stubbornly, the
index finger belongs in the butt and you look at the
name. What is it then? Being cordially present with
opinions, shouting students apart is something easy
and I know you. The opposite becomes
frighteningly large and there is no mercy, everyone
drinks. The rain is part of it, the silence is the main
component of the mood, beautiful and ugly, it's
good. An earworm spreads incessantly in the head.

There is no mercy. A considerable mind does not give up. He does not irritate other fine minds. To listen is a courtesy. To be soon gone again. To find the good hour. What do you need to ask? Don't lose your counterpart. Otherwise, they'll close. Or at least move on. My sore feet need a bath. The calluses are softening. Take a deep breath and experience it all again. Nothing is free and you have to pay for it. Take care of the slowly dying body with sensitivity. I am waiting for you and you will not come. And the freedom you believe in does not exist. Believe in it anyway. And grow old in the process. The feet are getting wrinkled. The heat is getting to my head. I haven't been happy for a long time. Friends ring my doorbell. I don't listen and my feet dissolve. Self-confidence is lost. The whole being collapses. Even strong thoughts are no longer helpful. And in the end, you have fun. And eventually gives up. The weeds and lettuce sprout, we have added enough fertilizer and are ready for anything. The cramp in the left side of your face slowly subsides, you may have accidentally sucked on the artificial fertilizer and get sick from it. That's how it is with the rich harvest, not everything is always perfect, the desire for more is the basis. Look at the wildly growing field. Give the almost dead side of your face a good massage and start a discussion with the holistic thinkers. They buy into you and want to see interest and you should quickly give up your good face. Win and lose faster, you can get a cramp in the other half of your face or heart, but don't destroy yourself completely or you won't be able to pay interest. And the faith in everyday life disappears quickly, you also do not know the past, the business counts and the lucky charm is the fertilizer. Strengthen your life and find new masters, help each other, life brings indescribable profit and small pains become bearable. A fertile mind. I did not dare to say anything, hiding and enjoying my life, sniffing my own stench again and again. Maybe the bliss is there, go back again, right into the darkest hole, count off my thoughts and live them out. Play sloppy with words and manipulate and catch the vulnerable and find hope for the glorious future with words. Wake up briefly at night, look at the alarm clock and see a time you will soon forget. The unresolved problems of the day twitch in your muscles, you no longer have to think, you like the fast-paced world and you are quite successful with it. You can compare the few unknown messes with yourself and your own will certainly be intensively examined. You can speak up at any time and have a quick answer ready. Forget about your gaps, starting tomorrow you won't have any anymore and you won't be here on earth, but underground. Or have you already become perfect?

An eternal Buddha kill

Finally the end.